THINGS YOU SHOULD

10

KNOW ABOUT

SPIDERS

By Steve Parker
Illustrated by
Richard Draper

Miles
Kelly
PUBLISHING

1 Fierce spiders

Spider facts

- The Sydney funnelweb lives in Eastern Australia.
- Its head and body are 4 to 5 centimetres long.
- It can live for more than five years.

Some spiders are very shy. If you go too near, they hide in a dark corner. The **FUNNELWEB SPIDER** of Australia may do this – or it may rear up, show its big fangs, and get ready to strike.
This is very dangerous.
The funnelweb is a big, strong spider, and its bite can kill a person.

Prey get trapped by the outer silk threads and the spider poisons them with its bite.

The funnelweb feeds at night on insects trapped by its silk threads. It feels for its food in the dark with its long front legs.

Spider danger!

Where poisonous spiders live, never put your hands into holes or corners. Use a stick to lift rocks or plants. Wear gloves and boots.

The threads make a funnel shape that leads to the spider's lair – a hole under a rock or root.

2 Wonderful webs

All spiders can make silk threads, but not all spiders make webs from them. The **ORB-WEB SPIDER** weaves a beautiful web shaped like a wheel. It has strong, straight threads, which look like the spokes on a wheel, and sticky spiral threads to catch the spider's prey.

Spider facts
- Orb-web spiders live all over the world, especially in woods and hedges.
- They are usually 1 to 3 centimetres in length.

New from old!

The orb-web spider makes a new web each day. First, it eats the old one, to recycle it. This means less new silk has to be made.

Long, straight threads give the web strength.

Spiral threads are soft, stretchy and sticky. Flies and moths just can't escape from them.

The whole web takes about one hour to build.

If the spider has just eaten, it will wrap up any new prey in silk threads, and store it at the web's edge. This is a snack for .... later on!

The spider waits in the middle of the web. When a victim gets caught and struggles, the spider feels the threads pull with its feet. It follows the tugs to find its meal.

3 Spiders can swim!

Spider facts
- The water spider lives in ponds, lakes and ditches in Europe and parts of Asia.
- Its head and body are 1.5 centimetres in length.

Few spiders live in water. In fact, there's only one! The **WATER SPIDER** breathes air like other spiders. By bringing small air bubbles under the water, this spider uses them to make a bigger bubble. This bubble home provides the spider with air.

The spider spins a dome of silk threads tied to water plants and pebbles. These trap the big bubble of air.

The big bubble or 'air bell' is the water spider's home. It stays inside most of the time. It eats, rests, and even breeds there.

The spider visits the surface to gather air. It traps small air bubbles between its legs and in its body hairs. It carries them underwater to add to the big bubble.

The spider pokes its legs out of the bubble to see if it can catch tadpoles, insects and tiny fish. It dashes out to bite them, and brings them back to eat.

Sea spider

The sea spider looks like a spider and lives in the sea. But it is not a real spider, just a close cousin.

4 Spiders can be deadly

Spider facts

- Black widows live in warm parts of the world.
- They are found in many habitats, from grasslands to gardens.
- The head and body are 1.3 centimetres in length.

All spiders have a poisonous bite, to kill prey or stop it struggling. But only a few spiders have poison powerful enough to harm a person. One which does is the **BLACK WIDOW**. It is small, shiny and black, and its bite can kill a human. So can its close cousin, the redback spider.

New for old!

All spiders grow by casting off, or moulting, their 'skin' — the old body case. There's a new, bigger one underneath.

The female black widow is usually the one which harms people. If she feels threatened, she tries to hide or run away. But sometimes she has to bite in self defence.

After mating the female may eat the male! This is why she is called the black 'widow'. She no longer has a partner.

The female black widow is larger than the male. She has a red mark shaped like an '8' on the underside of her body.

5 Big, hairy spiders

Spider facts

- Big, hairy tarantulas and bird-eating spiders live in tropical places.
- The head and body are up to 12 centimetres in length.
- The legs measure more than 25 centimetres across.

The biggest spiders in the world are hairy and huge – bigger than your hand. These **TARANTULAS** or bird-eating spiders really do eat birds, especially baby birds in nests. They also hunt insects, worms, and even lizards, mice and baby rats!

This female tarantula is guarding her eggs. They are surrounded by a shell, or cocoon, of silk. When the babies hatch, they look like tiny versions of their mother.

As dusk falls, the tarantula sets off to hunt. Most types prowl around on the ground, but some actually live in trees.

Spider hands!

Put on an old pair of gloves and stick two buttons to the thumbs. Link your thumbs together and walk like a tarantula!

Tarantulas have huge fangs which can bite very hard. But most are not especially poisonous. They rely on their strength and size.

13

6 Some spiders spit!

Spider facts

- Spitting spiders grow to 1.2 centimetres.
- They live in all regions except Australia and New Zealand.

SPITTING SPIDERS don't spit ordinary spit. They squirt a sticky liquid, like glue, from their fangs. This sprays over their prey like a rope or net. The prey gets tangled up and stuck down. Then the spitting spider moves in, delivers its poison bite, and begins to feed.

The spitting spider has only six eyes, not eight like other spiders.

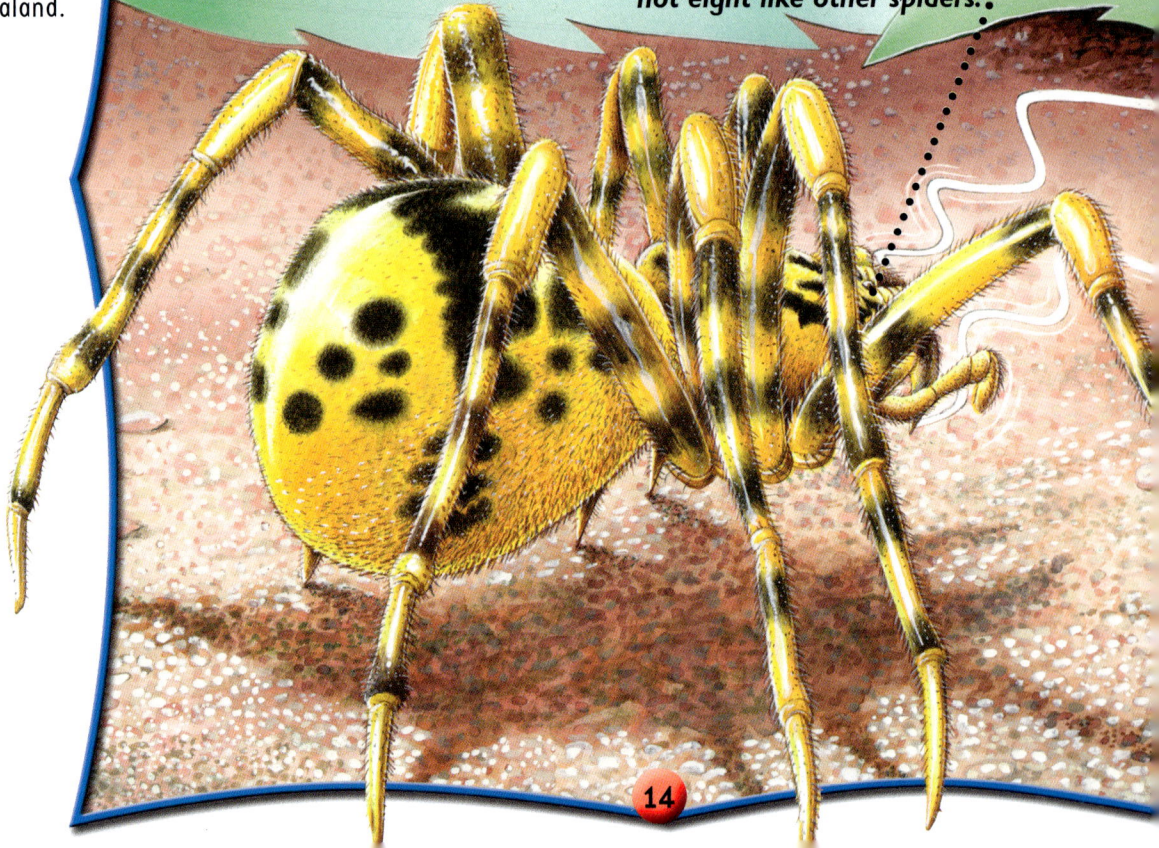

14

Spitting spiders catch tiny insects such as ants, flies, gnats and midges.

The spit becomes thick and sticky as soon as it comes out of the spider's fangs.

Spitting spiders often hunt on fences and walls around houses.

The spider shakes its head from side to side as it sprays. So the spit forms two wavy, zig-zag ropes that fall onto the victim and pin it down.

Spitting distance

The spitting spider can spit three times its own length!

Spider facts
- Raft spiders live in marshes, swamps and ponds around the world.
- Most are large, with a head and body up to 4 centimetres long.

The **RAFT SPIDER** sits on a leaf or stone, at the edge of a pond or marsh. Its front legs dip in the water and detect the tiny ripples of small creatures moving nearby. The spider dashes across the water, grabs its victim, and races back to land to eat its meal.

Raft spiders are big enough to grab young fish, water insects, pond snails, tadpoles and even small frogs.

The raft spider feels for its prey with its front legs and also with its palps – these look like short legs on either side of the fangs.

16

The spider's hairy body, legs and feet trap tiny bubbles of air. These stop the spider sinking under the water's surface.

Fishing for flies!

Fish for flies using a magnet, string and paper clips with paper 'wings'. The 'flies' stick to the magnet if you're quick enough!

17

8 Wearing disguises

It's not the flower that kills — it's the **CRAB SPIDER** hiding there. This spider is coloured and shaped to look like part of the flower. Blending into the surroundings like this is called camouflage. Many spiders do it. They look like leaves, bark, twigs and even bird droppings!

Crab spiders have wide bodies, and they walk sideways too — just like real crabs at the seaside.

Many little creatures visit flowers, such as bees, flies, beetles and ants. The crab spider eats them all! It has strong poison for its size. It surprises the visitor with a sudden bite which quickly causes death.

Crabs of many colours!

Crab spiders come in many colours, from white, yellow and pink, to red, green and grey. They always sit in a flower of the same colour.

The crab spider keeps very still, until the victim is close enough to bite.

9 Speedy hunter

Spider facts
- Wolf spiders live in most regions, among leaves and grass.
- The head and body are about 1–2 centimetres in length.

The **WOLF SPIDER** does not weave a web. It is a hunter and chases after victims, like a tiny version of a real wolf. It uses its eight big eyes to see, and its eight long legs to run fast.

The wolf spider hunts mainly by sight. Its very large eyes point forwards, for a good view of its prey.

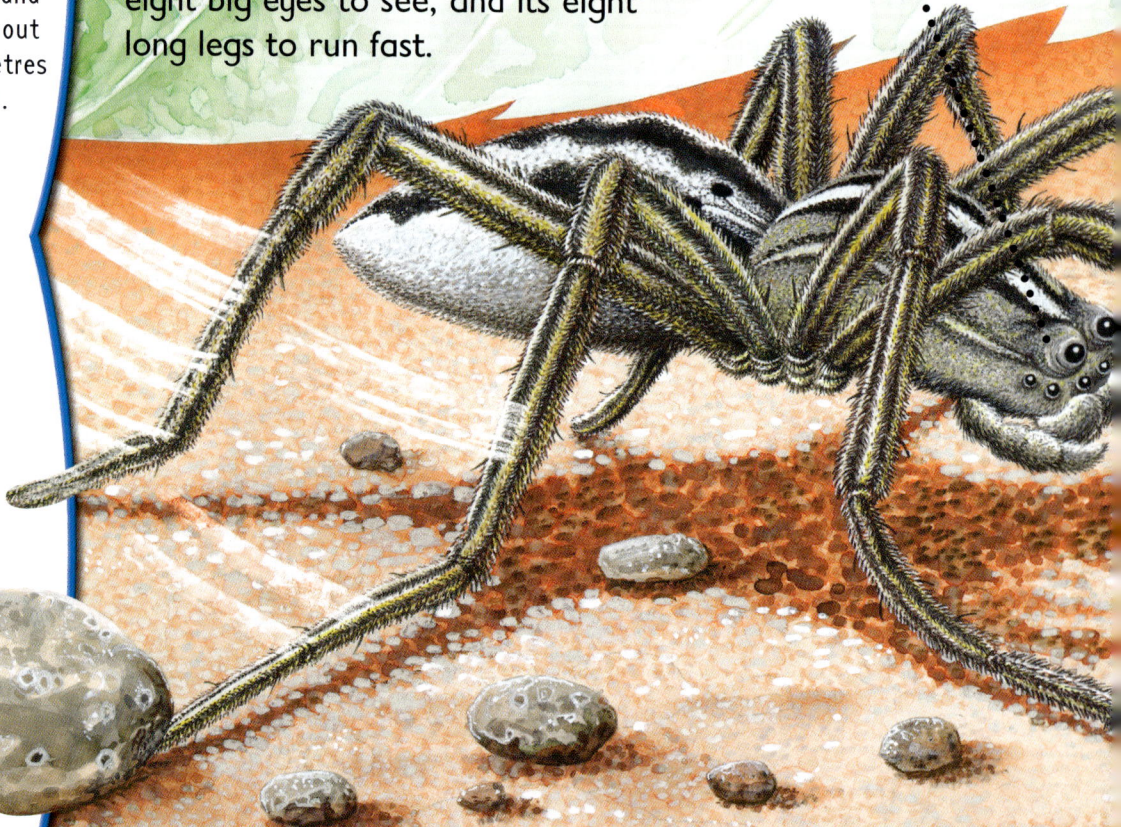

All spiders have a large head, with eight legs attached, and a rounded body. The wolf spider's head and body are small, but its legs are very long and strong.

Wolf spiders sunbathe on pebbles, soil or leaves before they hunt.

The wolf spider eats any creature it can catch, from a slow slug to a leaping cricket..

Making babies!

The female wolf spider lays eggs and wraps them all in a silk case for protection. A few weeks later, the baby spiders hatch.

10 Spiders hate baths!

Spider facts

- House spiders live in outbuildings, homes and sheds.
- The head and body are up to 2 centimetres in length.

HOUSE SPIDERS don't go in the bath to get clean. They prowl about at night, go too near the edge of a bath or sink, and slide in by accident. They can't climb back out because the walls are too steep and slippery. They need help!

The palps feel the way.

The fangs seize and bite prey.

Save a spider!

Put a glass over the spider, slide card under it and lift the card and glass together. Put the spider outside. If you can't do this – ask someone who can!

House spiders are helpful. They eat flies, mosquitoes and other pests. If there's one in the bath or sink – save it!

House spiders spin untidy-looking webs in corners. The sheet-like web is triangle-shaped. It's called a cobweb.

Index